HATSHEPSUT
THE MOST POWERFUL WOMAN PHARAOH

ANCIENT HISTORY 4TH GRADE
CHILDREN'S ANCIENT HISTORY

BABY PROFESSOR
EDUCATION KIDS

Speedy Publishing LLC

40 E. Main St. #1156

Newark, DE 19711

www.speedypublishing.com

Copyright 2017

IN THIS BOOK, WE'RE GOING TO TALK ABOUT THE LIFE OF HATSHEPSUT. SO, LET'S GET RIGHT TO IT!

WHO WAS HATSHEPSUT?

Hatshepsut was one of the most powerful female pharaohs of ancient Egyptian civilization. Her reign lasted for about two decades and many historians believe she was one of the most successful leaders of Egypt.

STATUE OF QUEEN HATSHEPSUT

PYRAMIDS IN EGYPT

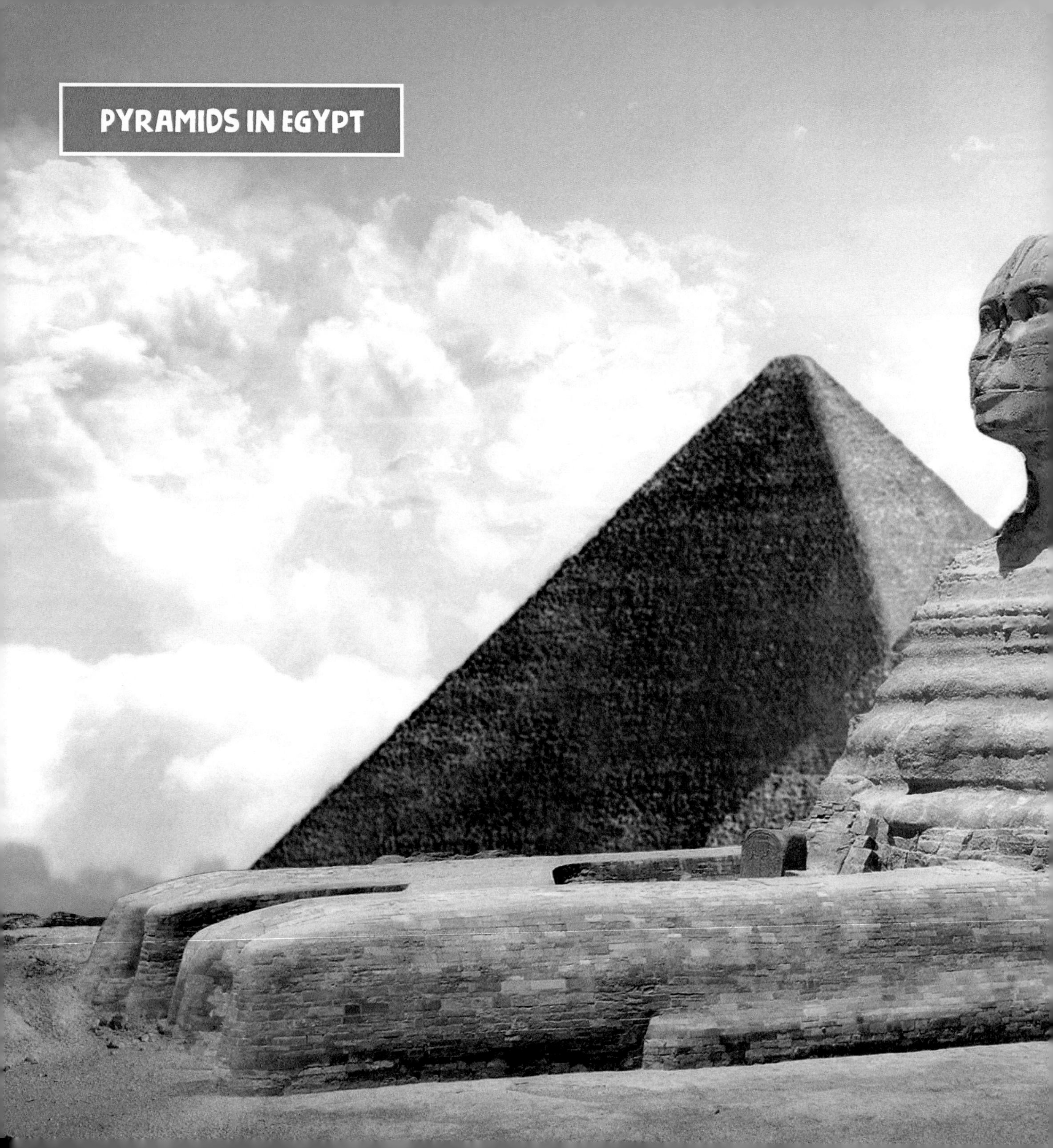

HATSHEPSUT'S EARLY LIFE

In the Egyptian culture, the pharaohs were almost all men and they had many wives. They sometimes also had women partners who were not their wives, but who gave them children. A pharaoh's child may have been in line to become pharaoh depending on which wife gave birth to the child. The rights to the throne for a particular child could also depend on whether there were other children who might have rights.

Hatshepsut was born around 1508 B.C. and her father was Thutmose I, who was pharaoh of Egypt. Her mother was Ahmose, her father's main wife. Because of her parents, Hatshepsut was expected to be queen when she grew up and be married to a pharaoh. Thutmose I died when Hatshepsut was twelve years of age.

THE OBELISK OF THUTMOSE I

STATUE OF THUTMOSE II

Hatshepsut's father had also fathered Thutmose II, not with Ahmose, Hatshepsut's mother, but with another less important wife. After the death of her father, Hatshepsut and her half-brother Thutmose II were married. This practice seems very strange, but in Egyptian culture this was a commonplace practice. It was meant to ensure that the royal bloodline would continue with those who were in the royal families.

During her husband's reign as pharaoh, Hatshepsut was his main wife and the Queen of Egypt. Thutmose II didn't accomplish much during his reign and there's some evidence that whatever he did achieve was motivated by his wife, Hatshepsut.

HATSHEPSUT AND NEFERURE'S BLOCK STATUE

HATSHEPSUT'S RISE TO POWER

Thutmose II, Hatshepsut's husband and half-brother, ruled as Pharaoh for 15 years. Then, he passed away. It was not unusual for people to die in their thirties during that time period. Hatshepsut wasn't yet 30-years-old and she was a widow. Their only child was a daughter Neferure.

Thutmose II had a male heir, but he was still a baby who had been born to a woman by the name of Isis who hadn't been his wife. This baby was now given the royal name of Thutmose III. He was Hatshepsut's stepson.

STATUE OF ISIS

ANCIENT RUINS

Since Thutmose III was still a baby, Hatshepsut took on the role of regent. A regent is someone who helps someone else rule a country. She was performing as regent for a while, but then, after seven years, she took over the role of pharaoh. No one knows exactly why she did this.

Some historians believe that there might have been a threat to the throne from other members of the royal family. Others believe that Hatshepsut was very ambitious so she seized the opportunity for power.

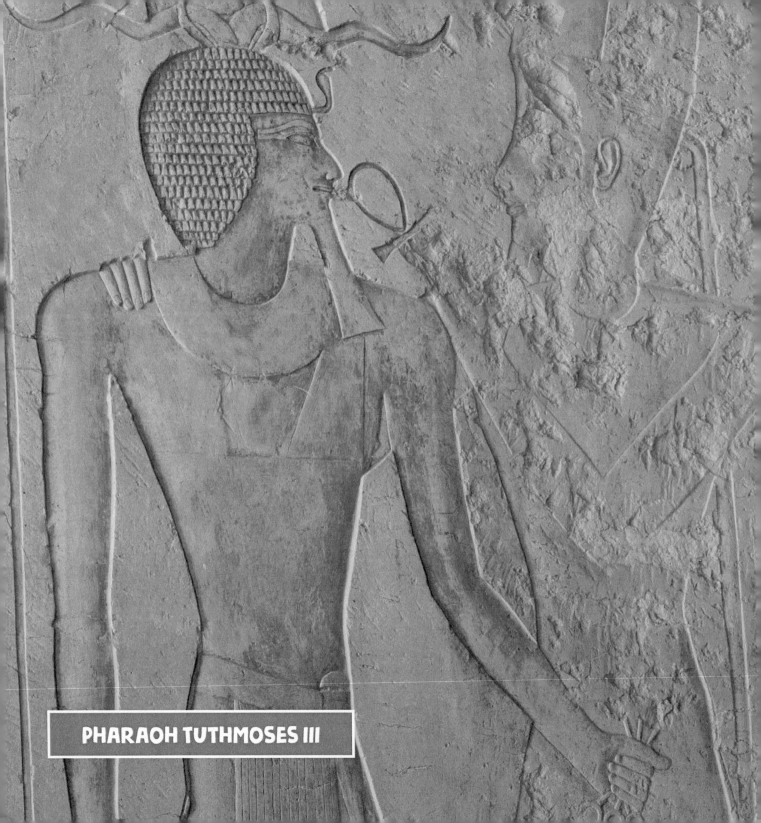

PHARAOH TUTHMOSES III

She never took the crown from Thutmose III and eventually he was ruling as well, but she took over as pharaoh, which placed him in a secondary position.

To establish that she had the right to be pharaoh, Hatshepsut emphasized her royal birth and stated that her father had proclaimed that she should succeed him in power. She began wearing the traditional kilt and pharaoh's crown just as a male pharaoh would wear. Sometimes the statues that were made of her showed a beard that was fake and depicted her as having a man's body.

FEMALE PHARAOH HATSHEPSUT WITH A FAKE BEARD

However, not all of her images were done this way. Others showed her in traditional female clothing. Historians believe that she controlled her image to appear like a man's so that the Egyptian people would consider her to be their leader and an authority figure. They don't believe that she was trying to trick anyone.

In order for Hatshepsut to gain power, she had to have the support of men in Egypt's government who would assist her in her role as pharaoh. She chose to recruit men who had been supportive of her father, Thutmose I. She also chose one of her favored stewards, who was named Senenmut. During Hatshepsut's reign, Senenmut became very powerful, so some historians believe that the two had a romantic relationship, but no one knows for sure.

STATUE OF SENENMUT

CLEOPATRA

HATSHEPSUT'S REIGN

Throughout the 3,000 years of history in Egypt, Hatshepsut was the third woman who had become pharaoh and she was the first to gain the full power of the position. It wasn't until 14 centuries after her rule that another powerful woman pharaoh by the name of Cleopatra was able to obtain the same level of power.

Historians believe that Hatshepsut must have been intelligent as well as cunning to order to remain in power. Hatshepsut reigned for over 20 years and during her leadership the civilization of Egypt thrived and became wealthy. Instead of conquering new territories and waging war, she worked to make the kingdom prosperous during a time of peace.

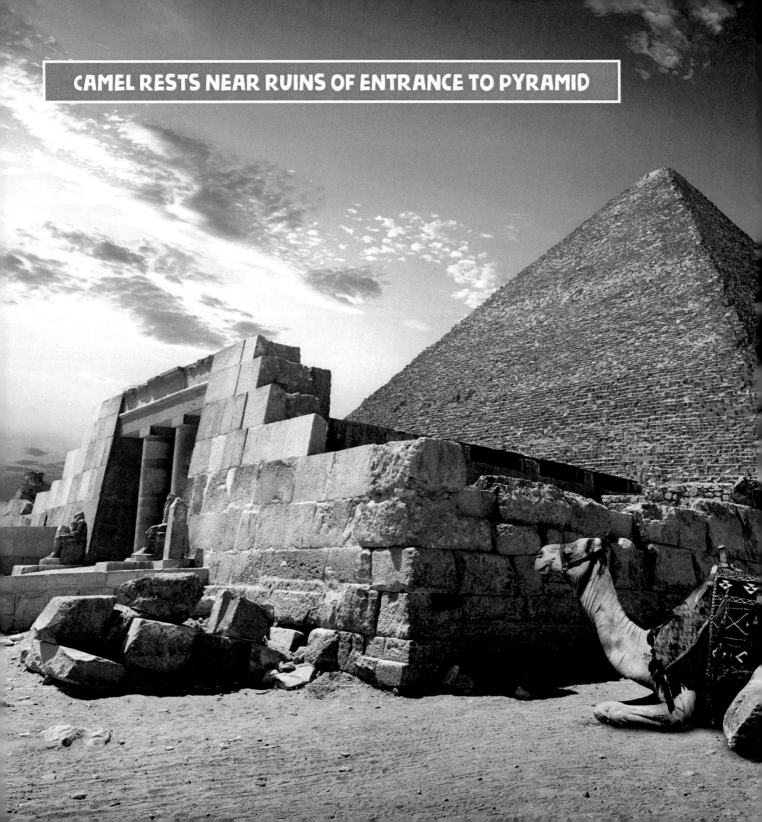

CAMEL RESTS NEAR RUINS OF ENTRANCE TO PYRAMID

She established many active trade and commerce relationships with other lands. She also concentrated on building projects and reconstructing monuments throughout the land of Egypt as well as in the nearby land of Nubia.

The temple that Hatshepsut had constructed at Deir el-Bahri for her own burial can still be seen today. The art and architecture had a softer and more delicate appearance than previous Egyptian works. The elegant temple rises from the landscape close to the Nile River. A long ramp goes up at a slope as it travels from a courtyard filled with trees and dotted with small pools to a landing terrace.

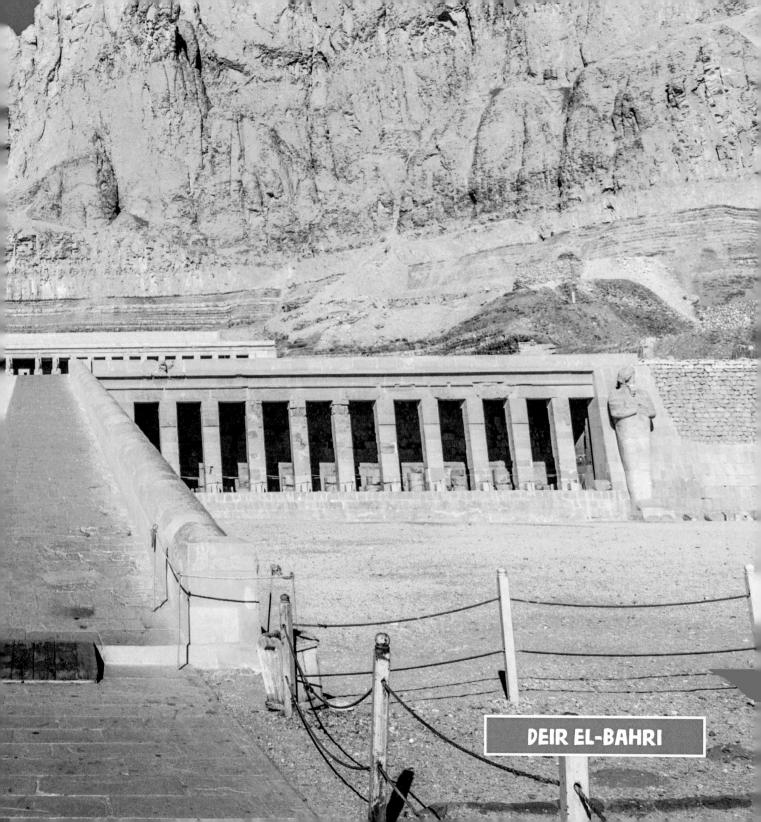

DEIR EL-BAHRI

Some of the trees in this courtyard were brought from Punt, which is modern-day Somalia. They are the first known tree transplants that came from one nation and then were planted in another. These trees can still be seen as fossils in the courtyard today.

The building was constructed with two levels of columns. The Greeks used their first columns a thousand years after these were constructed and Hatshepsut's temple was a turning point in Egyptian architecture. The temple is decorated with statues and inscriptions. The burial chamber designed for her was carved from the cliffs behind the building.

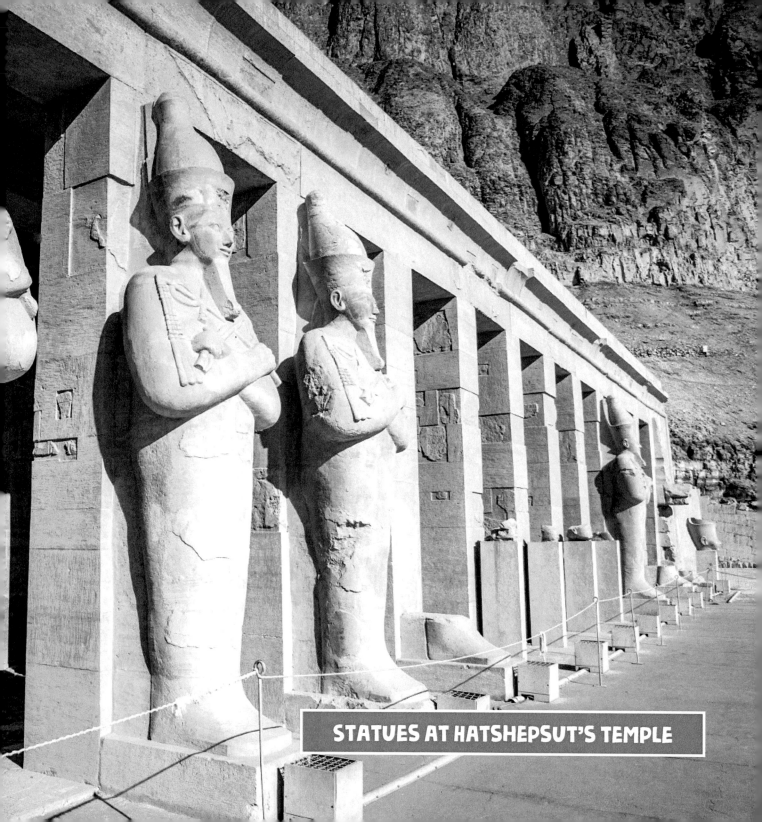

STATUES AT HATSHEPSUT'S TEMPLE

Her temple was so respected and admired that the pharaohs who ruled after her wanted to be buried nearby so this land eventually became described as the Valley of the Kings because of its many burial chambers.

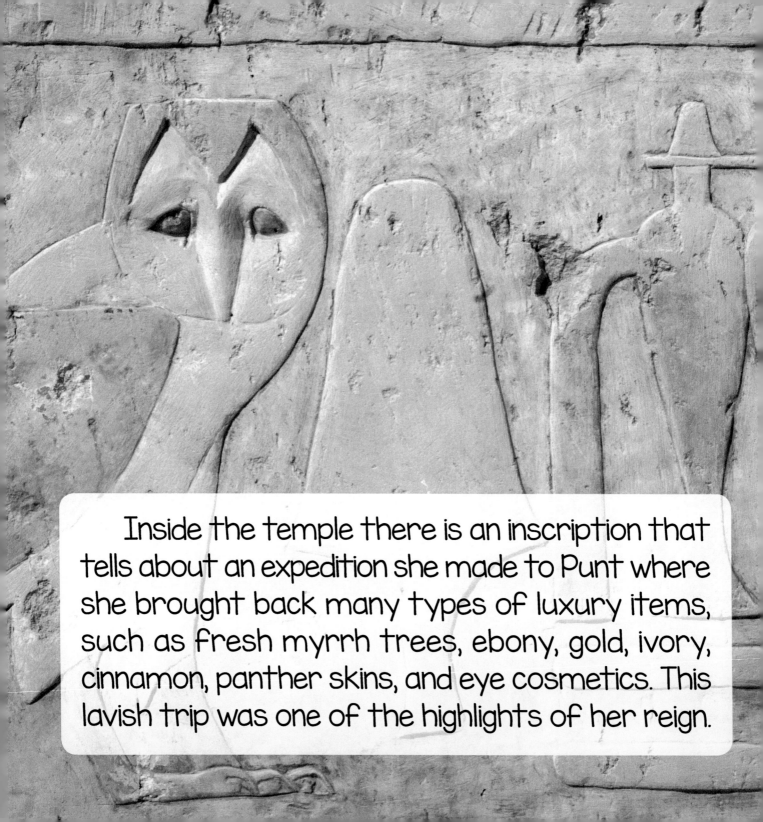

Inside the temple there is an inscription that tells about an expedition she made to Punt where she brought back many types of luxury items, such as fresh myrrh trees, ebony, gold, ivory, cinnamon, panther skins, and eye cosmetics. This lavish trip was one of the highlights of her reign.

PAINTING AT THE TEMPLE OF HATSHEPSUT

KARNAK TEMPLE

Except for the Pharaoh Ramesses II, she built on a larger scale than any other pharaoh who had come before her as well as those who reigned after her. In Karnak, she had two massive obelisks erected. In fact, she had so many pieces of art constructed that most museums around the world today that have Egyptian art have some artifacts from her reign.

Hatshepsut's reign lasted from 1478 B.C. to 1458 B.C.

THUTMOSE III COMES TO POWER

Hatshepsut passed away in the early part of 1458 B.C. Since the exact date of her birth isn't known, historians believe she was in her late forties. Her father's sarcophagus, the coffin for his mummified body, was reburied in her tomb. Her stepson, Thutmose III, became pharaoh.

THUTMOSE III

STATUES OF THUTMOSE III

He had been handling military affairs for quite some time and when he became pharaoh he was a great warrior. He also had construction work done on a grand scale as his stepmother had.

He went on to rule Egypt for another 30 years. Toward the end of his reign, he had many of the images of his stepmother destroyed. No one knows for sure why this was done. Thutmose III could have hated or resented his stepmother for taking power when he was a child. Perhaps he and the other leaders were concerned that other women would try to seize power and become pharaohs.

A third reason could be because he wanted to ensure that his heirs would be a clear line of succession when he died. Because of this planned destruction of her images, ancient Egyptologists didn't know much about her reign until they decoded the hieroglyphics on the wall at her burial temple.

In the year 1903, the famous British archaeologist Howard Carter found her sarcophagus, but her mummy was not inside. In 2005, an archaeological team began looking for her mummy and it was found in 2007. Today the mummified body of Hatshepsut is located in the Egyptian museum in the city of Cairo.

HOWARD CARTER

A STRONG FEMALE LEADER

Hatshepsut was the pharaoh of Egypt for 20 years. At the beginning, she was queen to her half-brother and husband Thutmose II. After he passed away, she became regent for her stepson, Thutmose III. Eventually, she claimed the role of pharaoh. Her reign was one of peace and prosperity. She constructed many beautiful buildings and took a luxury expedition during her reign. After she died, her stepson ruled as pharaoh for 30 years and eradicated many of the statues that showed her image. No one knows exactly why he attempted to destroy her legacy.

Now that you've learned about the life of Hatshepsut, you may want to read about the men and women of Ancient Egypt in the Baby Professor book Men and Women Were Equals in Ancient Egypt! History Books Best Sellers.

Made in the USA
San Bernardino, CA
16 May 2018